The Currency of the Dead

The Currency of the Dead

Matthew Petchinsky

1

The Currency of the Dead: Trading with Spectral Bankers

By: Matthew Petchinsky

Disclaimer

This book is a **creative and metaphysical exploration of spiritual commerce**—a living framework that unites the forces of wealth, death, and energetic exchange within the unseen worlds. It is intended as a work of **esoteric education, spiritual practice, and contemplative study** designed to support personal transformation through symbolic, ritual, and energetic understanding.

The Currency of the Dead: Trading with Spectral Bankers does **not** provide financial, business, legal, or investment advice. All references to "currency," "bankers," or "trading" describe **energetic and spiritual mechanisms** that symbolize the flow of life-force, reciprocity, and karmic balance—not literal economic or institutional systems.

The rites, sigils, meditations, and symbolic processes presented in this text are offered as **tools for personal empowerment, ancestral healing, and conscious energy management.** They are intended for sincere practitioners who understand that spiritual results are individual, experiential, and cannot be guaranteed or quantified.

Readers are encouraged to engage with discernment, grounding, and respect for their own safety, beliefs, and boundaries. The author and publisher accept no liability for personal interpretation, practice, or outcome.

This work is a **real metaphysical text**—a manual of living spirituality and sacred exchange—inviting readers to explore the deeper laws that govern value, vitality, and balance between the living and the unseen.

Introduction

Every transaction leaves an echo. Some echo in banks; others in bone.

We live in a world that believes currency begins and ends in numbers—an illusion of digits and decimals we call value. Yet behind every coin exchanged, every debt collected, and every inheritance received, something unseen moves: a current of energy older than economies and more binding than law. The ancients called it *reciprocity*, *karma*, *the breath of trade between worlds.* In the hidden markets beyond mortal eyes, the dead still balance their ledgers, ensuring that no wealth—spiritual or material—ever truly disappears.

The Currency of the Dead: Trading with Spectral Bankers invites you to peer into those unseen vaults. Within them dwell ancestral accountants, shadowed treasurers, and karmic auditors—entities that keep spiritual commerce flowing through generations. They are not demons nor deities in the conventional sense, but archetypal forces that govern balance. Where humanity sees wealth as possession, they see it as motion. To them, money, luck, and opportunity are forms of spirit that must circulate or rot.

In this book, you will learn to perceive wealth not merely as material gain, but as a vibration: a resonance shaped by the echoes of past actions, ancestral patterns, and energetic debts. When a family line suffers repeated poverty or misfortune, it is not always because of poor circumstance. Sometimes, the currency of the soul has been mismanaged—spent recklessly in lifetimes past, hoarded when generosity was required, or bound to contracts never consciously made. These debts whisper through time until someone in the living world hears the echo—and chooses to renegotiate it.

Here, negotiation does not mean submission. It means acknowledgment. By engaging with the spectral bankers—the symbolic custodians of energy flow—you learn to *audit your karmic accounts* and rewrite the contracts that govern your prosperity. You discover that abundance is neither a miracle nor a punishment, but an alignment of circulation: give, receive, renew.

Throughout these pages, you will encounter rituals, sigils, and metaphysical frameworks designed not to summon spirits, but to *speak their language.* The goal is not to worship or fear them, but to understand their function within the architecture of existence. When you begin to view your life as an energy economy, every decision becomes a transaction of meaning. Every act of gratitude pays an unseen dividend. Every act of greed incurs an unseen fee.

The teachings within are drawn from the intersection of metaphysical philosophy, ancestral symbolism, and energetic psychology. They will show you how to trace your personal wealth lineage—both material and immaterial—and to identify where the flow has been blocked or distorted. Through practice and reflection, you will learn to reconcile debts not with gold, but with intention; not with sacrifice, but with awareness.

To read this book is to step into a vault lit by candles made of memory. The ledgers you find there are not written in ink but in experience. Each page records what you have taken and what you have given. By studying these records, you awaken the art of spiritual balance—the truest form of wealth.

Let this be your initiation into the markets that never close: the markets of the dead, where fortune is measured not in coins, but in consciousness. Your inheritance awaits.

Chapter 1: The Ledger Beyond Life — Understanding Karmic Economics and Inherited Energetic Accounts

The Hidden Economy of Existence

Every soul is born into a ledger not of its own making. Before the first breath, before the first cry, the energy of lifetimes past shapes the balance sheets of our destiny. These are not punishments or rewards—they are records. Every act of generosity becomes a deposit into the spiritual economy; every act of cruelty, a withdrawal. The cosmos itself is the ultimate accountant, ensuring that equilibrium endures across lifetimes, bloodlines, and dimensions.

In karmic economics, the energy we give and take never vanishes—it circulates. When we give love freely, we expand credit with the unseen. When we manipulate, hoard, or harm, we accumulate energetic debt. This isn't moral bookkeeping; it's vibrational symmetry. The universe mirrors the state of your transactions, returning experiences that reflect your internal balance.

Inherited energetic accounts flow through families and communities much like material wealth. An ancestor's unresolved greed, generosity, or sacrifice may echo into your own experiences with money, luck, and stability. The patterns of scarcity or abundance you encounter might not have begun with you—but through awareness, they can end with you.

The Law of Circulation

Energy must move. The spectral bankers—those archetypal forces of balance—enforce this cosmic rule. They ensure that nothing remains stagnant. If abundance stops flowing through a lineage, it is often because fear, guilt, or ancestral wounds have frozen the current. Recognizing these blockages begins the process of reclamation.

To live in harmony with karmic economics, you must learn to trade consciously: to know what you offer, what you owe, and what you wish to cultivate. Gratitude becomes currency. Forgiveness clears debt. Creativity invests energy in growth. By practicing awareness in your exchanges—whether emotional, material, or spiritual—you align yourself with the rhythm of prosperity that the unseen world honors most.

Visualization: ***The Ancestral Vault***

Purpose: To perceive and understand your inherited energetic accounts.

1. **Find Stillness:** Sit comfortably and close your eyes. Let your breath slow until it matches the pulse of your heartbeat. Imagine the room fading into darkness, leaving only you and the sound of your breathing.
2. **The Descent:** Visualize yourself walking down a spiral staircase made of obsidian and gold. Each step hums softly under your feet, carrying you deeper into the earth, deeper into memory.
3. **The Vault Doors:** At the bottom, you find massive doors engraved with ancestral symbols. Place your hand upon them. Feel warmth—recognition. The doors open with a whisper.
4. **Inside the Vault:** Rows of floating ledgers stretch into eternity, glowing faintly with spectral light. Some are gold (acts of generosity and love), others silver (wisdom and service), and a few are shadowed or locked (unresolved debts or forgotten pain).
5. **The Ancestral Banker:** From the far end of the vault, a figure cloaked in starlight approaches. It is neither male nor female—merely presence. It offers you a single glowing ledger with your name on the cover.
6. **The Reading:** When you open it, words rearrange themselves as feelings. You sense where you've inherited gifts—compassion, creativity, courage—and where old debts linger—fear, greed, guilt. Do not judge. Simply witness.
7. **The Balancing:** Say aloud: *"I acknowledge the records that made me. I now choose balance, gratitude, and circulation."*
8. **The Return:** The figure nods. The vault brightens until all light converges in your heart. When you open your eyes, feel grounded, clear, and at peace.

Repeat this visualization whenever you sense stagnation or unexplained patterns in your finances, relationships, or confidence. It helps you access ancestral insight while staying rooted in conscious awareness.

Meditation: ***Balancing the Soul Ledger***
Duration: 15–20 minutes

1. **Preparation:** Light a candle or hold an object of value—a coin, ring, or crystal. Let it symbolize your exchange with life.
2. **Breath of Balance:** Inhale through the nose for four counts, imagining receiving energy. Exhale through the mouth for six counts, imagining releasing energy. Continue until the rhythm feels natural.
3. **Focus:** With each breath, visualize golden light flowing in on the inhale, silvery-blue light flowing out on the exhale. You are balancing giving and receiving.
4. **Statement of Alignment:** Repeat silently:
   "I am a vessel of flowing wealth. What I give returns in greater harmony. What I owe transforms into wisdom."
5. **Emotional Audit:** As you meditate, allow emotions related to money, success, or worth to surface. Observe them like entries in your soul's ledger—no guilt, no pride, just data.
6. **Transmutation:** When a heavy feeling arises, imagine it dissolving into radiant mist and being absorbed by your higher self. You are converting energetic debt into understanding.
7. **Closure:** After several minutes, imagine stamping the page of your inner ledger with the sigil of balance—two interlocking circles of light. Feel peace as the ink seals your intention.
8. **Return:** Slowly open your eyes. Take a deep breath and note any sensations of clarity or relief.

This meditation teaches the principle that awareness itself pays what is owed. Consciousness is the only currency that cannot be counterfeited.

10 Journal Prompts

1. What early memories shaped your understanding of money, generosity, or debt?
2. In what ways do you feel you "owe" others—emotionally, materially, or spiritually?
3. Are there patterns of financial or emotional struggle in your family that seem to repeat?
4. What qualities (discipline, gratitude, creativity) feel like inherited "credits" in your lineage?
5. When have you felt unworthy of receiving? Where might that belief have originated?
6. What moments in your life felt like energetic turning points—times when giving or withholding changed everything?
7. How does your body react when you think about abundance or lack? (Describe sensations, tensions, or warmth.)
8. If you could speak directly to your ancestral banker, what would you ask about your current life balance?
9. What fears surface when you imagine true financial and spiritual freedom?
10. Write an affirmation that redefines your wealth in energetic terms, such as: *"I am the flow that renews itself through giving, gratitude, and awareness."*

Closing Reflection

The first lesson of *The Currency of the Dead* is awareness. The ledgers of spirit are not hidden to punish—they are hidden because few dare to look. Once you do, you discover that nothing in your life is accidental. Every echo of fortune or misfortune is an invitation to renegotiate your energy with the universe.

To understand karmic economics is to see that wealth is not earned by effort alone—it is awakened by equilibrium. When you learn to balance what you inherit and what you create, you become your own banker in the realm beyond life.

Chapter 2: The Tomb Bankers — Spirits That Maintain the Flow Between Material and Immaterial Assets

The Gatekeepers of Circulation

In the invisible vaults of the afterlife, there exist entities known as **Tomb Bankers** — custodians of energy who ensure that spiritual and material wealth remain in motion. These are not "gods" or "ghosts" in the fearful sense, but *architects of balance*. They oversee exchanges between the living and the dead, ensuring that generosity is rewarded with continuity and greed is countered with stagnation.

Where mortal bankers count coins, **Tomb Bankers count vibrations**. They measure the flow of gratitude, reciprocity, and emotional energy behind every act of exchange. When your physical resources (money, possessions, or health) stagnate, it is often a sign that the immaterial accounts have been neglected — that the unseen current has stopped circulating.

The Tomb Bankers operate under a singular law: **Wealth must move**. Hoarded energy decays. Given energy multiplies. To work with these spectral treasurers, you do not "summon" them but align with their principles — rhythm, fairness, and respect. Through ritual, visualization, and meditation, you can open channels of exchange that allow your material prosperity to mirror spiritual abundance.

Understanding the Tomb Bankers' Function
Each Tomb Banker specializes in a form of energy flow:

- **The Keeper of Gold Dust** — Oversees the transmutation of material resources into creative opportunity.
- **The Auditor of Shadows** — Manages ancestral debts and forgotten promises.
- **The Curator of Breath** — Tracks the vitality you give through work, art, and emotion.
- **The Treasurer of Rest** — Converts stillness and gratitude into renewal and inspiration.

When you work with them symbolically, you are not worshiping these forces — you are acknowledging the *balance between giving and receiving*. Their "currency" is attention, awareness, and intention.

Ritual Offering: ***The Ceremony of Circulation***

Purpose: To honor the Tomb Bankers and reopen the flow between material and immaterial wealth.

Timing: Perform during the waxing moon (symbol of expansion) or at dawn when light first reenters the world.

Materials:

- A silver or copper bowl (representing shared wealth)
- A handful of rice or coins (symbolizing stored value)
- A lit candle (representing living energy)
- A small piece of bread, fruit, or honey (an offering to the unseen)
- A notebook or parchment (your "statement of intent")

Steps:

1. **Prepare the Space:** Clean the surface where you will perform the ritual. Set your bowl in the center, place the candle behind it, and the offering beside it.
2. **Ground Yourself:** Breathe deeply. On each inhale, imagine drawing up gold light from the earth; on each exhale, imagine sending silver light into the sky.
3. **Invocation:** Say aloud, slowly and with calm authority:
   "Spirits of circulation, keepers of energy's eternal exchange,
   I honor your balance, I respect your flow.
   May all that I give return renewed,
   May all that I withhold be released."
4. **Offering:** Place the rice or coins into the bowl. Whisper something you are ready to release — a fear of lack, guilt about money, or resentment toward success. Then add the bread, fruit, or honey, saying:
   "I feed the flow that feeds me."

5. **Statement of Intent:** On your parchment, write one sentence defining your desired balance between giving and receiving. Example: *"May my material efforts mirror my spiritual generosity."* Place this under the bowl.
6. **Closing:** Gaze at the candle flame. Visualize it becoming a portal of golden motion — the Tomb Bankers accepting your gesture and setting your energy into circulation. Whisper gratitude, then let the candle burn safely until it extinguishes naturally.
7. **After the Ritual:** Dispose of the offering respectfully outdoors or in flowing water. Keep the bowl clean for future ceremonies.

Meaning: This ritual reminds the subconscious that wealth is not accumulation but motion. The Tomb Bankers respond to sincere gestures of exchange, not desperation or greed.

Visualization: ***The Chamber of Echoing Coins***

Purpose: To sense the flow between your physical prosperity and your unseen energy.

1. **Begin in Stillness:** Close your eyes. Visualize yourself walking through a corridor lined with glowing vault doors made of stone and light. Each door hums with an ancestral tone.
2. **The Central Chamber:** You enter a grand hall filled with countless floating coins. Each coin reflects a moment when you gave or received — a kindness, a purchase, a sacrifice. The coins are your life's transactions, suspended in timeless motion.
3. **The Tomb Bankers Appear:** Four figures emerge — one cloaked in silver, one in gold, one in blue, and one in black. They move with measured grace, collecting the coins and tossing them gently into the air.
4. **The Flow:** When they move, energy begins to circulate. The coins swirl like galaxies, merging light and shadow. You feel the current enter your chest, pulsing with the rhythm of breath.
5. **The Exchange:** One Banker steps forward, handing you a single coin etched with your name. On one side it reads "GIVE," on the other "RECEIVE." You turn it over several times, understanding the equilibrium between both.
6. **Integration:** The Banker places the coin in your heart. The hall glows brighter. You sense your energy field balancing—neither grasping nor losing, only circulating.
7. **Return:** When the light fades, imagine walking back up the corridor to the waking world, carrying the rhythm of circulation with you.

Perform this visualization whenever you feel blocked financially, emotionally, or creatively.

Meditation: ***Breathing the Flow Between Worlds***
Duration: 15 minutes

1. **Setup:** Sit comfortably. Light a candle or keep a coin in your hand as a grounding anchor.
2. **Breath Pattern:** Inhale for 4 counts, hold for 2, exhale for 6. Continue until your body feels calm.
3. **Focus Phrase:** Silently repeat:
   "What I breathe in, I receive. What I breathe out, I give."
4. **Visualization:** With each inhale, imagine drawing soft golden mist from the realm of spirit — wealth energy descending. With each exhale, visualize sending silvery mist back — gratitude and giving ascending.
5. **Energetic Alignment:** As you continue, imagine your breath becoming a bridge between worlds. See faint outlines of the Tomb Bankers moving along this bridge, keeping balance with gentle gestures.
6. **Awareness:** Observe thoughts of lack, greed, or fear arise. Do not reject them. See the Tomb Bankers collect them like old coins and melt them into light, returning harmony to your inner economy.
7. **Completion:** Whisper: *"The flow between worlds moves through me, fair and unbroken."* Let the breath return to normal and sit in silence for a few minutes before opening your eyes.

10 Journal Prompts

1. How do you define *wealth* beyond money? What forms of abundance do you already possess?
2. Where in your life does energy feel stagnant — in finances, relationships, or creativity?
3. What "interest" are you paying emotionally for old mistakes or debts (guilt, shame, regret)?
4. What does the idea of "Tomb Bankers" symbolize to you personally?
5. Write about a time when giving freely led to unexpected returns. What does that teach you about flow?
6. Which of the four archetypes (Keeper of Gold Dust, Auditor of Shadows, Curator of Breath, Treasurer of Rest) do you resonate with most, and why?
7. What might the *currency* of your soul be—what energy or skill do you offer that enriches others?
8. Describe a ritual or daily action that could keep your energy circulating healthily.
9. What fears arise when you imagine letting go of control over money or outcomes?
10. Write an affirmation that harmonizes material and spiritual wealth, such as:
    "As I honor the flow of energy in all forms, prosperity honors me."

Closing Reflection

The Tomb Bankers are reminders that **spiritual commerce** is never separate from daily life. Every breath, every exchange, every act of giving or receiving contributes to the vast economy of existence. When you approach the world as both a participant and a steward of this energy, scarcity dissolves into rhythm.

To honor these spectral custodians is to respect motion itself. In their vaults, wealth never dies—it transforms. And when you learn to move with that current, both your material and immaterial accounts will always remain in balance.

Chapter 3: Debt of the Departed — Reclaiming Ancestral Wealth Lost Through Trauma and Fear

The Weight of Forgotten Accounts

Some inherit gold. Others inherit silence. But most of us inherit something far subtler — *an emotional and energetic balance sheet shaped by the unfinished business of those who came before us.*

Every lineage carries stories of survival: wars endured, migrations made, betrayals swallowed, loves lost, and fortunes destroyed. These experiences do not vanish when the body does. They crystallize into *energetic imprints* that flow through the generations, coded into the psyche like an invisible inheritance. When we encounter recurring hardship, financial instability, or a deep fear of loss, it is often the whisper of **ancestral debt** echoing through our own choices.

This chapter teaches how to recognize those echoes, trace their origins, and *reclaim* the power that trauma has frozen. By transforming inherited fear into conscious flow, you awaken dormant prosperity that was once locked away by pain.

Understanding Ancestral Debt

Ancestral debt is not about morality — it's about **energetic interruption**. When an ancestor suffers an experience too overwhelming to process — famine, betrayal, imprisonment, poverty, or shame — their survival instinct seals that pain away. The energy they once invested in courage, creativity, or trust becomes bound to the trauma itself.

Over time, descendants inherit not the memory, but the *pattern*. You may feel it as:

- A chronic fear of losing everything even when you are safe.
- Self-sabotage when prosperity approaches.
- A deep loyalty to struggle — as if wealth feels like betrayal.
- An unexplained guilt when things go well.

These are symptoms of an unpaid spiritual balance — an emotional loan taken out by survival itself. The goal is not to blame ancestors, but to *complete* what they could not. Healing the debt means reintroducing circulation where fear halted it.

The Three Layers of Ancestral Loss

1. **Material Displacement** — when wealth, land, or opportunity was taken through injustice or disaster. The energy of safety is replaced by vigilance.
2. **Emotional Imprint** — when shame or grief becomes a family's emotional currency, traded instead of love or expression.
3. **Spiritual Disconnection** — when an ancestor's despair causes a break in faith, creativity, or ritual — severing the current of inspiration that fuels prosperity.

You may carry one or all three. Recognizing which layer affects you most is the first step to liberation.

The Ritual of Reclamation: ***The Silent Audit***

Purpose: To identify and reclaim wealth energy lost through ancestral trauma.

Timing: Perform during the waning moon or on an evening when you feel emotionally reflective.

Materials:

- A black or deep-blue candle (to reveal what is hidden)
- A bowl of salt water (for purification)
- A mirror (to serve as the ancestral portal)
- A coin or small object inherited or symbolic of wealth
- A pen and paper

Steps:

1. **Ground Yourself:** Sit before the candle and mirror. Light the candle and place the salt water before it. Breathe slowly, sensing your roots extend into the earth.
2. **Invocation:** Whisper:
   "I call upon the line of those who came before,
   whose work, pain, and courage flow within me.
   I honor you not with sorrow, but with continuation."
3. **The Mirror's Truth:** Look into the mirror. Imagine your face shifting through layers of time — the features of ancestors appearing and fading like reflections in water.
4. **The Acknowledgment:** Say aloud:
   "To those who lost what could not be recovered — I see you.
   To those who feared wealth, I release your fear.
   To those who carried shame, I return it to the earth as wisdom."
5. **The Offering:** Dip your fingers into the salt water and touch the coin or chosen object. Feel its cool weight as you say:
   "The energy of wealth returns now purified.
   What trauma bound, I now redeem."

6. **Integration:** Close your eyes. Visualize threads of golden light rising from beneath the earth — ancestral energy returning through your lineage, flowing into your chest.
7. **Completion:** When ready, write any insights or images that arose. Let the candle burn safely to its end. Dispose of the salt water outdoors, symbolizing the release of pain back to nature.

The Psychology of Fear and Inheritance

Trauma teaches the nervous system that *safety is temporary.* When this belief becomes embedded across generations, descendants unconsciously replicate behaviors that match that energy — scarcity, self-denial, or overcontrol. The Tomb Bankers from Chapter 2 would call this "frozen capital": wealth energy trapped in old fear cycles.

To thaw it, one must create **emotional liquidity** — moments where trust outweighs fear, where giving outweighs guarding. Each time you practice gratitude, share resources, or take a courageous step toward growth, you are releasing ancestral assets from energetic storage.

Visualization: ***The River Beneath the Graveyard***

Purpose: To reconnect with ancestral abundance hidden beneath loss.

1. **Begin:** Close your eyes. Imagine standing in a quiet graveyard under a twilight sky. The air hums faintly — not of sorrow, but of memory.
2. **The Descent:** Kneel and place your hands on the soil. Feel vibration beneath your palms, like water running deep underground.
3. **The Revelation:** The ground becomes transparent, revealing a vast golden river flowing beneath the graves. This is the *currency of the departed* — every unspent dream, every act of love never expressed, still shimmering in potential.
4. **The Exchange:** Lower a silver thread from your heart into the river. Whisper: *"I honor what you could not complete. I continue it in strength and clarity."*
5. **The Flow Returns:** The river responds, sending gentle light up through the thread into your chest. The warmth spreads through your heart, hands, and mind. You feel the emotional inheritance transforming into courage and creativity.
6. **Return:** When ready, the river's light fades, leaving a calm awareness. You rise, carrying the renewed flow of your lineage within you.

This visualization teaches that loss never erased the current—it merely submerged it. You are the one chosen to bring it back to the surface.

Meditation: ***Breath of Redemption***
Duration: 10–15 minutes

1. **Posture:** Sit with your hands over your heart. Inhale deeply for four counts, exhale for six.
2. **Focus:** As you breathe, silently repeat: *"With every breath, I redeem what was lost. With every exhale, I release what was never mine to carry."*
3. **Awareness:** Allow images or sensations connected to your family's history to arise. Observe without judgment.
4. **Transmutation:** When sadness or heaviness surfaces, imagine breathing golden light directly into it, converting it into wisdom.
5. **Completion:** When you feel light and balanced, bow your head slightly and say:
   "The debt is known. The flow is restored. The lineage breathes freely again."

10 Journal Prompts

1. What financial or emotional fears seem to "run in the family"?
2. Describe an ancestor or family story where loss or shame surrounded money or success.
3. When did you first feel responsible for someone else's suffering or security?
4. What emotions arise when you imagine surpassing your family's historical level of wealth or comfort?
5. If fear had a voice inherited from your lineage, what would it say?
6. What would it look like to live in a way that *honors* your ancestors but doesn't repeat their pain?
7. How do you define redemption — not as forgiveness, but as restoration of flow?
8. What new "family wealth" (values, creativity, generosity) are you ready to build from this healing?
9. What symbols or objects in your home carry ancestral energy? How might you cleanse or empower them?
10. Write an affirmation of liberation, such as:
    "I am the living continuation of my ancestors' unfulfilled prosperity. Their struggle ends in my strength, their fear transforms into my freedom."

Closing Reflection

The **Debt of the Departed** is not punishment — it is a request. The spirits of those who came before you are not haunting you with lack; they are asking for closure. They long for someone to understand that their fear was not failure, but unfinished motion.

When you answer that call, you do not merely heal your lineage — you **reopen the current** that sustains creation itself. The wealth that returns is not only financial; it is the restoration of trust, creativity, and vitality. The ancestors do not demand repayment in gold. They seek remembrance in courage — the courage to thrive where they could not.

In reclaiming their lost fortune of faith and flow, you become the *living vault of redemption*, carrying prosperity that echoes both forward and backward through time.

Chapter 4: Negotiating with the Veiled Investors — Creating Balanced Offerings to Spectral Patrons

The Unseen Marketplace of Exchange

There is a law older than money, older than temples: **all gain requires exchange.** The ancients knew this truth instinctively. When they reaped from the soil, they gave thanks with grain. When they sought wisdom, they offered silence. When they desired power, they offered responsibility.

In the spiritual economy explored in *The Currency of the Dead*, this same principle governs every invisible transaction. To receive energy from the spectral realm — inspiration, protection, opportunity, or renewal — something of value must move in return. This is not bribery or superstition. It is **symmetry**. The spirits you align with, known as the *Veiled Investors*, do not seek worship — they seek circulation.

They are the unseen patrons of balance — archetypal intelligences that invest in human potential. Their "returns" are measured not in gold, but in how well you embody purpose, generosity, and mastery. When you stagnate, their investment diminishes; when you evolve, their dividends grow. This chapter reveals how to negotiate consciously with these forces, ensuring mutual respect and sustainable abundance between worlds.

Who Are the Veiled Investors?

The Veiled Investors are not demons, gods, or ancestors, but *archetypal currents of exchange*. They manifest differently depending on what kind of energy you are cultivating:

- **The Patron of Momentum** — fuels new beginnings, projects, and ventures when you commit fully.
- **The Keeper of Equilibrium** — stabilizes your flow when chaos or greed distort balance.
- **The Whisperer of Innovation** — invests in creativity, invention, and daring expression.
- **The Curator of Legacy** — ensures your work endures beyond your lifetime, aligning with ancestral continuity.

They are "veiled" because they do not appear visibly — their language is synchronicity, intuition, and opportunity. When you give them attention, they respond with alignment: doors open, clarity returns, and timing improves.

However, neglect or overreliance distorts the pact. A proper relationship is **contractual through awareness** — every act of receiving must be matched with an act of gratitude or restoration.

The Philosophy of Spectral Negotiation

To negotiate with the unseen, you must first understand that *energy respects boundaries*. Spirits do not require obeisance; they require coherence. A vague, desperate offering will yield confusion. A clear, confident offering creates flow.

Negotiation begins by asking yourself:

1. What do I genuinely seek — stability, insight, renewal, wealth, healing?
2. What am I willing to offer in equal vibration — discipline, creativity, service, or reverence?
3. What outcome will honor both myself and the forces that aid me?

When you can answer these questions honestly, you enter sacred commerce — not supplication, but collaboration.

The Offering Equation

Every offering consists of **three elements**:

1. **Intent** – The clear statement of purpose. What energy are you requesting or returning?
2. **Representation** – The symbolic form through which energy moves (object, action, time, or attention).
3. **Integration** – The way you embody the exchange afterward — through choices, gratitude, and behavior.

An unbalanced offering—too lavish or too empty—disturbs the flow. The goal is to mirror natural law: give precisely enough to create movement, not depletion.

Ritual: ***The Pact of the Silver Veil***

Purpose: To establish conscious, balanced connection with the Veiled Investors — spirits of exchange who help manifest opportunities while keeping energy in circulation.

Timing: Best performed on a Thursday (day of expansion and prosperity) or during the first quarter moon.

Materials:

- A silver or white cloth (the Veil)
- One silver coin or reflective object
- A white candle
- A small offering of water, tea, or wine
- A written statement of intent

Steps:

1. **Prepare the Space:** Lay the cloth on a clean surface. Place the coin at its center, symbolizing the point where material and immaterial meet. Light the candle above it.
2. **Center the Mind:** Breathe deeply, letting thoughts slow. Feel a calm neutrality — neither pleading nor commanding.
3. **State the Invitation:** Speak aloud:
   "To the Veiled Investors, patrons of exchange and balance,
   I open my energy to mutual prosperity.
   May my effort be met with opportunity,
   my gratitude with renewal."
4. **Present the Offering:** Pour the liquid into a small bowl beside the coin. As it ripples, imagine it carrying your sincerity into unseen realms. Say:
   "This is the current that binds all worlds — may it flow with integrity."

5. **Declare Your Intent:** Read your written statement aloud, beginning with "I offer..." and "I request..." For example:
   "I offer diligence, consistency, and gratitude. I request clarity in purpose and fruitful pathways for my creative work."
6. **Seal the Pact:** Pass your right hand slowly above the coin and candle flame, envisioning a silver veil forming between you and the unseen — translucent, respectful, alive with mutual trust.
7. **Closing:** Whisper:
   "As energy circulates, so too shall opportunity.
   As gratitude grows, so too shall grace."
   Extinguish the candle, fold the cloth over the coin, and keep it in a safe place for seven days. Afterward, store the coin somewhere meaningful (altar, wallet, workspace) as a talisman of partnership.

Visualization: ***The Hall of Mirrors and Markets***

Purpose: To understand the mutual nature of spiritual exchange and identify what you truly offer.

1. **Begin:** Close your eyes. See yourself standing in an endless hall of mirrors lit by candlelight. Each reflection of you is slightly different — some wealthier, some wiser, some weary. These are your possible selves, each shaped by your energetic investments.
2. **The Market Awakens:** Beyond the mirrors, stalls and tables appear. Spirits cloaked in shimmering veils trade luminous items — ideas, emotions, memories. The sound is not noise but harmony.
3. **The Investors Approach:** Four figures approach you, faces obscured by silver gauze. One holds a feather, one a book, one a seed, one a flame. Each represents a domain of exchange — inspiration, knowledge, growth, and vitality.
4. **The Contract of Breath:** They extend their hands. You inhale deeply, offering your breath as signature. They inhale in return. The air between you shimmers, sealing an unseen pact.
5. **The Lesson:** One of them whispers (in intuition, not words): *"We invest in what circulates through you. Keep your gifts in motion."*
6. **Return:** The market fades. You are left holding a single symbol — a light, a sound, or a memory. This is your energetic currency. Carry it consciously into your waking life.

Meditation: ***Balancing the Spiritual Portfolio***
Duration: 20 minutes

1. **Posture:** Sit comfortably with your spine straight. Place one hand on your heart, the other on your solar plexus.
2. **Breath Rhythm:** Inhale for four counts, hold for two, exhale for six. Continue until your heartbeat slows.
3. **Reflection:** Think of three ways you currently receive — money, praise, inspiration — and three ways you give — service, creativity, love.
4. **Visualization:** Imagine each inflow as golden light entering your chest; each outflow as silver light leaving your palms.
5. **Balancing Flow:** Allow both colors to merge into a radiant white equilibrium. Repeat silently:
   "I give in gratitude, I receive in grace. Flow remains unbroken."
6. **Awareness:** If guilt or imbalance arises ("I take too much," "I give too much"), visualize the Veiled Investors gently adjusting invisible scales before you until both sides level.
7. **Completion:** Whisper:
   "My worth is not in accumulation, but in harmony. The flow sustains us all."
   Sit in silence for several minutes before resuming normal awareness.

10 Journal Prompts

1. What does "exchange" mean to you beyond material trade?
2. Recall a moment when you received unexpected help or opportunity. How might that have been an unseen investment in you?
3. What gifts or talents flow most naturally through you — and how consistently do you share them?
4. Where might you be hoarding energy (time, attention, ideas) that wants circulation?
5. Which of the Veiled Investors (Momentum, Equilibrium, Innovation, or Legacy) resonates most with your current goals?
6. Write an "offering ledger": three things you commit to giving back for every blessing received.
7. What would a balanced, healthy relationship with abundance feel like in your body? Describe it physically.
8. How do you currently acknowledge unseen assistance — intuition, coincidence, timing?
9. When have you given too much without alignment or received without gratitude? What did that teach you?
10. Write an affirmation such as: *"My life is a contract of balance. I honor the unseen investors through generosity, clarity, and joy."*

Closing Reflection

Negotiating with the Veiled Investors is not about summoning supernatural benefactors — it is about engaging **the living principle of reciprocity.** Every breath you take is borrowed energy; every act of giving repays that debt in grace. When you build conscious partnerships with the unseen — through balanced offerings, ethical intent, and heartfelt gratitude — you become a **trusted steward** in the cosmos's vast marketplace.

The Veiled Investors do not demand worship. They respect clarity, integrity, and motion. When you live as both benefactor and beneficiary, you step into the true economy of spirit — one where wealth is never lost, only transmuted through the endless rhythm of giving and return.

Chapter 5: The Resurrection of Credit — Transforming Stagnation into Thriving Financial Life-Force

The Forgotten Pulse of Prosperity

Every current of wealth — from the flow of blood in the body to the circulation of money through markets — obeys the same law: **movement sustains life**. When energy stops, decay begins. Just as still water breeds disease, stagnant credit breeds fear, guilt, and paralysis. Yet beneath every moment of financial stagnation lies dormant vitality waiting to be revived.

This chapter unveils the metaphysical principle of **credit resurrection**: the art of reanimating frozen energy and converting it into living current. Credit, in its oldest sense, means *trust*. To "extend credit" is to invest belief that life will continue to flow. When you lose faith in yourself, the world mirrors that doubt — opportunities halt, abundance shrinks, and vitality dims.

Resurrecting credit means restoring the pulse of trust — in self, in circulation, in the unseen economy that responds to your alignment. It is not about debt forgiveness or external repair; it is about reviving **spiritual liquidity**, the capacity for life-force to move through you again.

Understanding Energetic Stagnation

Financial stagnation is rarely just circumstantial — it is *energetic congestion*. The channels of exchange between giving and receiving become blocked by one or more of the following:

- **Fear of failure or success** — halting flow through indecision.
- **Resentment of loss** — clinging to what no longer serves.
- **Guilt about desire** — suppressing natural creative hunger.
- **Exhaustion and over-giving** — draining reserves without replenishment.

These create what spectral economics calls **spiritual overdrafts**: not financial debt, but energy deficits. The aura dims, magnetism weakens, and synchronicities stop responding. The Tomb Bankers and Veiled Investors (introduced in earlier chapters) mark this as *inactivity of account*.

The cure is not more effort — it is circulation. When energy begins moving again, credit resurrects itself naturally, as trust is reestablished both within and without.

The Anatomy of Resurrection

To revive stagnation, three components must awaken:

1. **Recognition** – Acknowledging that stagnation is a teacher, not a punishment.
2. **Release** – Letting go of psychic clutter, outdated identities, and grudges.
3. **Reinvestment** – Channeling recovered energy into aligned motion: new projects, generosity, and creative expansion.

When these three converge, the spiritual economy reboots. You become your own **living bank**, generating and circulating vitality rather than waiting for external deposits.

Ritual: ***The Candle of Renewal***

Purpose: To transmute stagnation into flow and restore the energetic "credit line" between your inner and outer worlds.

Timing: Dawn on a Sunday or at the new moon — moments of rebirth.

Materials:

- One green or gold candle (symbol of prosperity's spark)
- A small bowl of clean water
- A few coins or stones (representing stored potential)
- A slip of paper and pen

Steps:

1. **Preparation:** Sit before the unlit candle. Take three deep breaths. On each exhale, imagine releasing tension from your chest — the place where trust resides.
2. **Naming the Stagnation:** On the paper, write a short sentence naming what feels blocked: *"Fear of taking risk," "Old debt shame," "Lack of creative drive."*
3. **Declaration:** Say aloud:
   "I recognize this stagnation as a teacher, not a master.
   Its lesson is complete. Its energy now transforms."
4. **The Lighting:** Light the candle and hold the paper close enough to feel warmth (but not to burn). Watch the flame flicker as a symbol of renewed movement.
5. **Activation:** Drop the coins or stones into the bowl of water, saying:
   "Flow returns. Credit breathes. Prosperity lives."
   Visualize the water swirling gently with golden light.

6. **Integration:** Dip your fingertips into the water and touch your forehead, heart, and palms — sealing flow in thought, emotion, and action.
7. **Closing:** Let the candle burn until it feels complete. Dispose of the water outdoors, symbolizing released energy returning to nature.

Repeat this ritual whenever you feel immobilized or fearful. Over time, it reconditions the nervous system to associate motion with safety instead of risk.

Visualization: ***The Heart as Treasury***

Purpose: To reconnect your inner vitality with the greater current of wealth and trust.

1. **Begin:** Close your eyes and visualize a great vault within your chest — ancient, carved from light and stone. Inside, countless golden threads pulse faintly. These are the unspent credits of your life-force.
2. **The Inspection:** Some threads may appear dull or knotted — these represent blocked energy. Approach them gently. Whisper: *"I remember you."* The knots loosen as you acknowledge them.
3. **The Resurrection:** From above, a shaft of sunlight pierces the vault, illuminating everything. The threads begin to glow brighter, weaving together into a radiant network.
4. **The Circulation:** See energy moving outward from your heart into your body — through arms, legs, and crown — and beyond, into your home, work, and community. The flow becomes rhythmic, like breathing.
5. **Completion:** Whisper: *"Trust restored, current renewed."* Feel your pulse synchronize with the rhythm of circulation — steady, alive, confident.

Meditation: ***Breathing the Credit Current***
Duration: 15 minutes

1. **Position:** Sit upright with both feet grounded. Place one hand on your chest, one on your abdomen.
2. **Rhythmic Breath:** Inhale for 4 counts — visualize drawing in glowing gold light (trust). Hold for 2 counts — feel stability. Exhale for 6 counts — release dull, grey energy (fear).
3. **Affirmation Cycle:**
    - On inhale: *"I receive life freely."*
    - On exhale: *"I release all that blocks its flow."*

    Continue until you feel warmth spreading through your hands.
4. **Expansion:** Imagine each breath widening your "credit line" of energy. See yourself surrounded by a gentle current of light that extends beyond the body — connecting you to opportunities, allies, and synchronicity.
5. **Integration:** Sit in silence and visualize one tangible action you will take within 24 hours to express this renewed trust — a conversation, a creative task, a small gesture of generosity.

This meditation turns faith into motion, the essence of credit resurrection.

Principles of Energetic Credit

1. **Trust is the currency of creation.** When you trust yourself, energy invests in you.
2. **Debt transforms through understanding, not avoidance.** Awareness converts shadow into wisdom.
3. **Generosity restarts the current.** Give what you can — a word, a service, a smile — and circulation begins anew.
4. **Rest is not withdrawal.** Stillness, when intentional, accrues interest in vitality.
5. **Every choice is a transaction.** Spend attention wisely; invest only in what expands your life-force.

10 Journal Prompts

1. Where in your life does stagnation feel most pronounced — finances, creativity, or relationships?
2. What beliefs about money or success have "frozen" your energy flow?
3. How has fear disguised itself as responsibility in your daily choices?
4. Recall a time when trust (in yourself or others) restored momentum. What changed afterward?
5. What emotions arise when you consider taking bold financial or creative steps?
6. Write a forgiveness statement to yourself or an ancestor for any perceived "failure" around money.
7. What could "prosperity as life-force" mean in your body — describe sensations, colors, or images.
8. How can you practice giving without depletion — what kind of generosity feels sustainable?
9. Name three small acts that would signal to the universe that you are ready to circulate again.
10. Write an affirmation such as:
    "I am the resurrection of credit — trust reborn, energy flowing, life thriving through me."

Closing Reflection

Resurrecting credit is the spiritual art of restoring **faith in flow**. It does not erase hardship; it converts it into momentum. Every setback, debt, or pause becomes compost for growth once you understand that stagnation is simply energy asking for redirection.

When you reclaim trust in yourself and the unseen systems that sustain existence, you no longer chase prosperity — you *embody* it. You become both lender and borrower in a single continuous circuit of gratitude and creation.

In this rebirth, wealth is not accumulation but respiration — each inhale a promise, each exhale an offering. The current moves, and with it, life itself awakens.

Appendix A: Ritual of the Golden Obol Exchange

Purpose of the Ritual

The **Golden Obol Exchange** is the culminating rite of *The Currency of the Dead*. It symbolizes the **moment when the living restores the balance of wealth energy between worlds** — paying respect to ancestral debts, renewing spiritual credit, and opening channels for abundance to flow freely once again.

The ritual's name originates from the *obol*, an ancient coin placed in the mouths of the departed to ensure safe passage into the afterlife. In this metaphysical adaptation, the obol becomes an **energetic currency** — a vessel of gratitude, trust, and restored reciprocity between material and immaterial realms.

The purpose is threefold:

1. **To honor the unseen bankers, ancestors, and investors who govern energy flow.**
2. **To release stagnant wealth energy** caused by fear, guilt, or imbalance.
3. **To awaken the living current of prosperity**, transforming it into a continuous circuit of giving and receiving.

The Golden Obol Exchange does not involve literal offerings to spirits in a dogmatic sense — rather, it's an **artistic, meditative ceremony** designed to help the practitioner realign with universal law: *all that flows returns magnified.*

Preparation and Setting

Timing: The ideal moment is at twilight — when day transitions to night — symbolizing exchange between seen and unseen. Perform during a waxing moon (growth) if you seek expansion, or during a waning moon (release) if you wish to dissolve debt and fear.

Location: Choose a quiet, clean space — a table, altar, or even a patch of earth. Dim lighting is preferred, as the ritual relies on the symbolic flicker between visibility and shadow.

Mindset: Approach with calm curiosity, not reverence or fear. You are not summoning; you are negotiating balance. The tone should be firm, respectful, and centered.

Materials Required

- **One gold-colored coin** (real, plated, or symbolic — this is your *obol*)
- **A glass or bowl of water** (symbol of flow and continuity)
- **A white or gold candle** (representing living energy)
- **A piece of paper and pen** (to record your "exchange declaration")
- **A small bowl of salt or soil** (symbolizing the physical realm)
- **Incense, herbs, or essential oil** (to represent the breath of circulation — sandalwood or cinnamon work well)

Optional: a mirror or polished object to represent reflection, allowing you to "see" both yourself and the unseen in equal measure.

The Stages of the Golden Obol Exchange

Stage I: The Acknowledgment of the Flow

1. **Cleansing Breath:** Take three deep breaths. Inhale through the nose, exhale through the mouth. Imagine each exhale clearing dust from a golden current that runs from your heart outward into space.
2. **Lighting the Candle:** As the flame steadies, whisper:
   "Here burns the currency of life — trust made visible."
   The flame is not worshipped; it is observed as motion incarnate.
3. **Touch the Coin:** Hold the obol in your right hand. Feel its temperature, weight, and texture. It represents every transaction — both physical and energetic — that you have ever made or will make.

Stage II: The Statement of Accounts

On your piece of paper, write three sections:

- **Debts Owed:** Not literal bills, but emotional or spiritual imbalances (e.g., "fear of receiving," "self-criticism when I succeed," "ancestral shame around money").
- **Debts Released:** Write what you consciously forgive — both what others owe you and what you no longer owe yourself.
- **Credit Renewed:** State the virtues and powers you now claim as living currency (e.g., "creative abundance," "stability through gratitude," "compassion as capital").

Read these three aloud slowly. With each line, visualize numbers in a glowing cosmic ledger rebalancing themselves — old entries closing, new ones appearing in light.

Say:

"All that was unbalanced finds its flow.
All that was stagnant begins again.
The ledgers of the dead and the living reconcile in harmony."

Fold the paper and place it beneath the candle.

Stage III: The Exchange

1. **The Water Offering:** Gently lower the coin (the obol) into the bowl of water. Listen to the faint sound it makes — that is the "currency entering circulation."
2. **Invocation:** Say:
   "To those who guard the passage of wealth through shadow and time — I offer this token of motion.
   May all debts transform into lessons,
   May all lessons become gifts,
   And may all gifts return multiplied in wisdom."
3. **Gesture of Return:** With your left hand, sprinkle a pinch of salt or soil into the bowl. This unites earth and water — symbol of grounding prosperity in the real world.

As the ripples spread, imagine an invisible network of light stretching from your bowl to countless unseen vaults and hearts — a universal treasury of shared abundance.

You are neither requesting nor begging; you are acknowledging **participation in the cosmic economy of flow**.

Stage IV: The Mirror of Reciprocity

If using a mirror, hold it up so you see both your reflection and the candlelight. Whisper:

"As I give, I receive. As I receive, I give. The circuit remains unbroken."

Visualize the golden light from the flame and the reflection merging into one — a halo of energy that encircles you. It symbolizes your renewed *credit line* with the universe: trust reestablished, energy circulating, opportunities forming.

Stage V: The Sealing and Integration

1. **Lift the Obol:** Remove the coin from the water. Dry it gently with a clean cloth.
2. **Declaration of Flow:** Say aloud:
   "This obol has crossed worlds and returned. Its value is eternal motion.
   I am the living current through which it now moves."
3. **Placement:** Keep the coin somewhere significant — your wallet, altar, or work desk. It now serves as a **symbolic bond** between your material actions and the metaphysical economy you have realigned with.
4. **Extinguish the Candle:** Whisper softly:
   "Balance sealed. Motion preserved."

Allow the ashes, water, or salt to return to nature — pour them into running water or scatter them on the soil. The exchange is complete when all materials are returned to their elements.

Optional Addendum: The Annual Renewal

The Golden Obol Exchange may be repeated once per year on **All Souls' Eve**, **Samhain**, or any personal anniversary of transformation. Each repetition strengthens your resonance with cosmic flow.

In successive years, you may wish to **add additional obols** to your ritual — one for each major life shift or new venture. These form your *Vault of Living Credit*, a tangible reminder of the evolution of your trust in the unseen.

Energetic Interpretation

- **The Candle:** Represents the human spirit — the flame that transforms density (wax) into illumination (heat and light).
- **The Coin in Water:** Symbolizes faith submerged in uncertainty — an act of surrender that leads to renewal.
- **Salt or Soil:** The grounding of wealth; the reminder that prosperity must serve tangible good.
- **The Mirror:** Conscious self-recognition — the reconciliation of giver and receiver.

These symbols work together to rewire subconscious beliefs about scarcity, worth, and permission to receive.

Affirmation of Completion

End the ritual by reading or memorizing this short invocation whenever you handle money, make decisions, or feel the pull of fear:

"I am the bridge between worlds.
The dead remember through me, the living flow because of me.
Gold moves where gratitude leads,
And I am forever solvent in the currency of light."

Closing Reflection

The **Golden Obol Exchange** is not merely a ceremony — it is a philosophy in action. It teaches that *value is movement*, and movement is sacred. Every coin you spend, every act of generosity, every creative impulse is an echo of this same exchange.

To live by its current is to live as both banker and borrower in the grand ledger of existence — where wealth is not measured by possession, but by the elegance of your circulation.

When you next find a coin glinting in the street, pause for a moment. It may be a reminder — a golden whisper from beyond — that the economy of spirit never truly closes. Only you decide how freely its light will move through your hands.

Appendix B: Sigils for Wealth Ancestry Repair

Across time, cultures have used sacred geometry and written symbols as keys to unseen forces. In *The Currency of the Dead*, sigils serve as **energetic contracts**—visual representations of intent that rewrite inherited financial trauma into balance and vitality.

This appendix teaches how to design and activate your own *Wealth Ancestry Repair Sigils*: personalized glyphs that symbolically mend the fractures within your lineage's prosperity current. These sigils are not meant for superstition, but for **focused meditation and subconscious re-patterning**—a language through which the psyche and ancestral field can communicate.

Philosophy of Wealth-Line Sigilcraft

Every family line carries vibrational stories of exchange: times of generosity, times of deprivation, times of fear. When you craft a sigil, you extract the *essence* of your chosen intention and give it shape. The design becomes a **visualized credit line**—a continuous circuit linking you, your ancestors, and the living universe of flow.

A true Wealth-Repair Sigil must express:

1. **Acknowledgment** – "I know the imbalance that was left unresolved."
2. **Redemption** – "I transform inherited fear into conscious trust."
3. **Circulation** – "I keep wealth moving through gratitude, not grasping."

Choosing the Intention

Begin with a short, present-tense statement that defines what you are restoring. Examples:

- "I release ancestral poverty."
- "Wealth flows freely through my bloodline."
- "Trust and generosity rebuild my family's fortune."

Keep the phrase simple, declarative, and emotionally charged. This sentence is your *energetic signature*—the phrase you will distill into symbolic language.

The Sigil Formula (Removing Vowels and Duplicate Consonants)

Traditional sigilists simplify words to compress their meaning into pure form. The process below converts language (a left-brain construct) into geometry (a right-brain expression).

1. **Write the full intention.**
   Example: *"Wealth flows freely through my bloodline."*
2. **Remove all vowels (A E I O U and Y if it acts as a vowel).*
   Result: WLTH FLWS FRLY THRGH MY BLLDLN
3. **Eliminate repeating consonants.** Keep only the first instance of each letter.
   Remaining letters: **W L T H F S R G M Y B D N**
4. **Combine the letters into an interwoven design.**
   - Begin by sketching each letter in stylized form.
   - Overlap and merge lines until no single character is recognizable, forming an abstract emblem.
   - Round sharp edges if you seek gentle flow; add angular lines if you seek decisive transformation.
5. **Enclose the sigil in a geometric frame** (circle, triangle, spiral, or infinity loop). The frame represents containment—the "vault" in which the new wealth current resides.

This technique converts linguistic meaning into symbolic resonance. The final form is **a condensed vibrational algorithm** for financial healing within your lineage.

Charging the Sigil (Activation)

Once drawn, the sigil must be **charged**—imbued with attention and emotion to ignite its current. Choose one or more of the following activation methods:

1. **Breath Method:** Gaze softly at the sigil and breathe rhythmically. With each inhale, imagine energy entering the symbol; with each exhale, see it radiating gold light. Continue until you feel warmth or a subtle pulse.
2. **Elemental Method:**
    - Pass the sigil briefly through incense smoke (Air).
    - Hold above candle flame for gentle heat (Fire).
    - Sprinkle with drops of clean water (Water).
    - Touch to salt or soil (Earth).

    These four gestures declare the sigil valid across all planes of matter.
3. **Emotional Charge:** Focus on gratitude as if the repair has already occurred. Emotion anchors the sigil in reality.

When you feel an internal *click*—a quiet certainty—the sigil is alive.

Integration and Release

After charging, decide whether to **display** or **release** the sigil:

- **Display:** Place it on your altar, near financial documents, or in a workspace. It continues to radiate its intention like an ancestral beacon.
- **Release:** Burn the sigil safely, bury its ashes in earth, or submerge it in flowing water. This sends the pattern into circulation, symbolizing that the universe now "remembers" the repair.

Whichever method you choose, end by saying aloud:

"The pattern is renewed.
The family current flows.
What was bound is now in motion."

Suggested Sigil Intention Templates

Below are sample intentions you may tailor before applying the removal-and-combination process:

1. **Lineage Prosperity** – "The wealth of my ancestors circulates through me in balance."
2. **Debt Liberation** – "All inherited scarcity transforms into creative strength."
3. **Trust in Flow** – "Money and energy return where gratitude dwells."
4. **Entrepreneurial Renewal** – "I manifest legacy income through inspired action."
5. **Generational Healing** – "Fear of fortune ends; wisdom of abundance begins."

Each of these phrases, once distilled into its consonantal code, becomes a unique *ancestral key*.

Meditative Use

To deepen the effect, meditate with your sigil once weekly for one lunar cycle (about 28 days):

1. Light a candle.
2. Gaze at the sigil until lines blur slightly.
3. Whisper your original statement in present tense three times.
4. Visualize golden energy streaming backward through generations, mending breaks in the family's prosperity web, then returning to you.

This repetition imprints the new pattern into the subconscious field shared by your lineage.

Ethical Considerations

Sigils amplify the *intention* behind them. They should never be crafted to take from others, dominate, or manipulate. True ancestral repair restores equilibrium—not excess at another's expense. Use your creations as meditative art, journaling tools, or talismans of self-trust, never as instruments of coercion.

Closing Reflection

When you reduce words to letters, and letters to shapes, you return to the original language of the cosmos: **pattern and rhythm**. Each Wealth Ancestry Repair Sigil you create is a small resurrection of that language—a signature declaring that your bloodline remembers how to circulate life, gratitude, and abundance.

Your ancestors wrote their stories in survival; you continue them in prosperity. The sigil is your shared autograph across time—a golden signature on the eternal ledger of flow.

Message from the Author:

I hope you enjoyed this book, I love astrology and knew there was not a book such as this out on the shelf. I love metaphysical items as well. Please check out my other books:

-Life of Government Benefits

-My life of Hell

-My life with Hydrocephalus

-Red Sky

-World Domination:Woman's rule

-World Domination:Woman's Rule 2: The War

-Life and Banishment of Apophis: book 1

-The Kidney Friendly Diet

-The Ultimate Hemp Cookbook

-Creating a Dispensary(legally)

-Cleanliness throughout life: the importance of showering from childhood to adulthood.

-Strong Roots: The Risks of Overcoddling children

-Hemp Horoscopes: Cosmic Insights and Earthly Healing

- Celestial Hemp Navigating the Zodiac: Through the Green Cosmos

-Astrological Hemp: Aligning The Stars with Earth's Ancient Herb

-The Astrological Guide to Hemp: Stars, Signs, and Sacred Leaves

-Green Growth: Innovative Marketing Strategies for your Hemp Products and Dispensary

-Cosmic Cannabis

-Astrological Munchies

-Henry The Hemp

-Zodiacal Roots: The Astrological Soul Of Hemp

- **Green Constellations: Intersection of Hemp and Zodiac**

-Hemp in The Houses: An astrological Adventure Through The Cannabis Galaxy

-Galactic Ganja Guide

Heavenly Hemp

Zodiac Leaves
Doctor Who Astrology
Cannastrology
Stellar Satvias and Cosmic Indicas
Celestial Cannabis: A Zodiac Journey
AstroHerbology: The Sky and The Soil: Volume 1
AstroHerbology:Celestial Cannabis:Volume 2
Cosmic Cannabis Cultivation
The Starry Guide to Herbal Harmony: Volume 1
The Starry Guide to Herbal Harmony: Cannabis Universe: Volume 2
Yugioh Astrology: Astrological Guide to Deck, Duels and more
Nightmare Mansion: Echoes of The Abyss
Nightmare Mansion 2: Legacy of Shadows
Nightmare Mansion 3: Shadows of the Forgotten
Nightmare Mansion 4: Echoes of the Damned
The Life and Banishment of Apophis: Book 2
Nightmare Mansion: Halls of Despair
Healing with Herb: Cannabis and Hydrocephalus
Planetary Pot: Aligning with Astrological Herbs: Volume 1
Fast Track to Freedom: 30 Days to Financial Independence Using AI, Assets, and Agile Hustles
Cosmic Hemp Pathways
How to Become Financially Free in 30 Days: 10,000 Paths to Prosperity
Zodiacal Herbage: Astrological Insights: Volume 1
Nightmare Mansion: Whispers in the Walls
The Daleks Invade Atlantis
Henry the hemp and Hydrocephalus

10X The Kidney Friendly Diet
Cannabis Universe: Adult coloring book
Hemp Astrology: The Healing Power of the Stars

Zodiacal Herbage: Astrological Insights: Cannabis Universe: Volume 2

Planetary Pot: Aligning with Astrological Herbs: Cannabis Universes: Volume 2

Doctor Who: Convergence Protocol – The Replicator War

Nightmare Mansion: Curse of the Blood Moon

The Celestial Stoner: A Guide to the Zodiac

Cosmic Pleasures: Sex Toy Astrology for Every Sign

Hydrocephalus Astrology: Navigating the Stars and Healing Waters

Lapis and the Mischievous Chocolate Bar

Celestial Positions: Sexual Astrology for Every Sign

Apophis's Shadow Work Journal: **:** A Journey of Self-Discovery and Healing

Kinky Cosmos: Sexual Kink Astrology for Every Sign

Digital Cosmos: The Astrological Digimon Compendium

Stellar Seeds: The Cosmic Guide to Growing with Astrology

Apophis's Daily Gratitude Journal

Cat Astrology: Feline Mysteries of the Cosmos

The Cosmic Kama Sutra: An Astrological Guide to Sexual Positions

Unleash Your Potential: A Guided Journal Powered by AI Insights

Whispers of the Enchanted Grove

Cosmic Pleasures: An Astrological Guide to Sexual Kinks

369, 12 Manifestation Journal

Whisper of the nocturne journal(blank journal for writing or drawing)

The Boogey Book

Locked In Reflection: A Chastity Journey Through Locktober

Generating Wealth Quickly:How to Generate $100,000 in 24 Hours

Star Magic: Harness the Power of the Universe

The Flatulence Chronicles: A Fart Journal for Self-Discovery

The Doctor and The Death Moth

Seize the Day: A Personal Seizure Tracking Journal

The Ultimate Boogeyman Safari: A Journey into the Boogie World and Beyond

Whispers of Samhain: 1,000 Spells of Love, Luck, and Lunar Magic: Samhain Spell Book

Apophis's guides:Witch's Spellbook Crafting Guide for Halloween

Frost & Flame: The Enchanted Yule Grimoire of 1000 Winter Spells

The Ultimate Boogey Goo Guide & Spooky Activities for Halloween Fun

Harmony of the Scales: A Libra's Spellcraft for Balance and Beauty

The Enchanted Advent: 36 Days of Christmas Wonders

Nightmare Mansion: The Labyrinth of Screams

Harvest of Enchantment: 1,000 Spells of Gratitude, Love, and Fortune for Thanksgiving

The Boogey Chronicles: A Journal of Nightly Encounters and Shadowy Secrets

The 12 Days of Financial Freedom: A Step-by-Step Christmas Countdown to Transform Your Finances

Sigil of the Eternal Spiral Blank Journal

A Christmas Feast: Timeless Recipes for Every Meal

Holiday Stress-Free Solutions: A Survival Guide to Thriving During the Festive Season

Yu-Gi-Oh! Holiday Gifting Mastery: The Ultimate Guide for Fans and Newcomers Alike

Holiday Harmony: A Hydrocephalus Survival Guide for the Festive Season

Celestial Craft: The Witch's Almanac for 2025 – A Cosmic Guide to Manifestations, Moons, and Mystical Events

Doctor Who: The Toymaker's Winter Wonderland

Tulsa King Unveiled: A Thrilling Guide to Stallone's Mafia Masterpiece

Pendulum Craft: A Complete Guide to Crafting and Using Personalized Divination Tools

Nightmare Mansion: Santa's Eternal Eve

Starlight Noel: A Cosmic Journey through Christmas Mysteries

The Dark Architect: Unlocking the Blueprint of Existence

Surviving the Embrace: The Ultimate Guide to Encounters with The Hugging Molly

The Enchanted Codex: Secrets of the Craft for Witches, Wiccans, and Pagans

Harvest of Gratitude: A Complete Thanksgiving Guide

Yuletide Essentials: A Complete Guide to an Authentic and Magical Christmas

Celestial Smokes: A Cosmic Guide to Cigars and Astrology

Living in Balance: A Comprehensive Survival Guide to Thriving with Diabetes Insipidus

Cosmic Symbiosis: The Venom Zodiac Chronicles

The Cursed Paw of Ambition

Cosmic Symbiosis: The Astrological Venom Journal

Celestial Wonders Unfold: A Stargazer's Guide to the Cosmos (2024-2029)

The Ultimate Black Friday Prepper's Guide: Mastering Shopping Strategies and Savings

Cosmic Sales: The Astrological Guide to Black Friday Shopping

Legends of the Corn Mother and Other Harvest Myths

Whispers of the Harvest: The Corn Mother's Journal

The Evergreen Spellbook

The Doctor Meets the Boogeyman

The White Witch of Rose Hall's SpellBook

The Gingerbread Golem's Shadow: A Study in Sweet Darkness

The Gingerbread Golem Codex: An Academic Exploration of Sweet Myths

The Gingerbread Golem Grimoire: Sweet Magicks and Spells for the Festive Witch

The Curse of the Gingerbread Golem

10-minute Christmas Crafts for kids

Christmas Crisis Solutions: The Ultimate Last-Minute Survival Guide

Gingerbread Golem Recipes: Holiday Treats with a Magical Twist

The Infinite Key: Unlocking Mystical Secrets of the Ages

Enchanted Yule: A Wiccan and Pagan Guide to a Magical and Memorable Season

Dinosaurs of Power: Unlocking Ancient Magick

Astro-Dinos: The Cosmic Guide to Prehistoric Wisdom

Gallifrey's Yule Logs: A Festive Doctor Who Cookbook

The Dino Grimoire: Secrets of Prehistoric Magick

The Gift They Never Knew They Needed

The Gingerbread Golem's Culinary Alchemy: Enchanting Recipes for a Sweetly Dark Feast

A Time Lord Christmas: Holiday Adventures with the Doctor

Krampusproofing Your Home: Defensive Strategies for Yule

Silent Frights: A Collection of Christmas Creepypastas to Chill Your Bones

Santa Raptor's Jolly Carnage: A Dino-Claus Christmas Tale

Prehistoric Palettes: A Dino Wicca Coloring Journey

The Christmas Wishkeeper Chronicles

The Starlight Sleigh: A Holiday Journey

Elf Secrets: The True Magic of the North Pole

Candy Cane Conjurations

Cooking with Kids: Recipes Under 20 Minutes

Doctor Who: The TARDIS Confiscation

The Anxiety First Aid Kit: Quick Tools to Calm Your Mind

Frosty Whispers: A Winter's Tale

The Infinite Key: Unlocking the Secrets to Prosperity, Resilience, and Purpose

The Grasping Void: Why You'll Regret This Purchase

Astrology for Busy Bees: Star Signs Simplified

The Instant Focus Formula: Cut Through the Noise

The Secret Language of Colors: Unlocking the Emotional Codes

Sacred Fossil Chronicles: Blank Journal

The Christmas Cottage Miracle

Feeding Frenzy: Graboid-Inspired Recipes

Manifest in Minutes: The Quick Law of Attraction Guide

The Symbiote Chronicles: Doctor Who's Venomous Journey

Think Tiny, Grow Big: The Minimalist Mindset

The Energy Key: Unlocking Limitless Motivation

New Year, New Magic: Manifesting Your Best Year Yet

Unstoppable You: Mastering Confidence in Minutes

Infinite Energy: The Secret to Never Feeling Drained

Lightning Focus: Mastering the Art of Productivity in a Distracted World

Saturnalia Manifestation Magick: A Guide to Unlocking Abundance During the Solstice

Graboids and Garland: The Ultimate Tremors-Themed Christmas Guide

12 Nights of Holiday Magic

The Power of Pause: 60-Second Mindfulness Practices

The Quick Reset: How to Reclaim Your Life After Burnout

The Shadow Eater: A Tale of Despair and Survival

The Micro-Mastery Method: Transform Your Skills in Just Minutes a Day

Reclaiming Time: How to Live More by Doing Less

Chronovore: The Eternal Nexus

The Mind Reset: Unlocking Your Inner Peace in a Chaotic World

Confidence Code: Building Unshakable Self-Belief

Baby the Vampire Terrier
Baby the Vampire Terrier's Christmas Adventure
Celestial Streams: The Content Creator's Astrology Manual
The Wealth Whisperer: Unlocking Abundance with Everyday Actions
The Energy Equation: Maximize Your Output Without Burning Out
The Happiness Algorithm: Science-Backed Steps to Joyful Living
Stress-Free Success: Achieving Goals Without Anxiety
Mindful Wealth: The New Blueprint for Financial Freedom
The Festive Flavors of New Year: A Culinary Celebration
The Master's Gambit: Keys of Eternal Power
Shadowed Secrets: Groundhog Day Mysteries
Beneath the Burrow: Lessons from the Groundhog
Spring's Whispers: The Groundhog's Prediction
The Limitless Mindset: Unlock Your Untapped Potential
The Focus Funnel: How to Cut Through Chaos and Get Results
Bold Moves: Building Courage to Live on Your Terms
The Daily Shift: Simple Practices for Lasting Transformation
The Quarter-Life Reset: Thriving in Your 20s and 30s
The Art of Shadowplay: Building Your Own Personal Myth
The Eternal Loop: Finding Purpose in Repetition
Burrowing Wisdom: Life Lessons from the Groundhog
Shadow Work: A Groundhog Day Perspective
Love in Bloom: 5-Minute Romantic Gestures
The Shadowspell Codex: Secrets of Forbidden Magick
The Burnout Cure: Finding Balance in a Busy World
The Groundhog Prophecy: Unlocking Seasonal Secrets
Nog Tales: The Spirited History of Eggnog
Six More Weeks: Embracing Seasonal Transitions
The Lumivian Chronicles: Fragments of the Fifth Dimension
Money on Your Mind: A Beginner's Guide to Wealth
The Focus Fix: Breaking Through Distraction

January's Spirit Keepers: Mystical Protectors of the Cold
Creativity Unchained: Unlocking Your Wildest Ideas in 2025
Manifestation Mastery: 365 Days to Rewrite Your Reality
The Groundhog's Mirror: Reflecting on Change
The Weeping Angels' Christmas Curse
Burrowed in Time: A Groundhog Day Journey
Heartbeats: Poems to Share with Your Valentine
Dino Wicca: The Sacred Grimoire of Prehistoric Magick
Courage of the Pride: Finding Your Inner Roar
The Lion's Leap: Bold Moves for Big Results
Healthy Hustle: Achieving Without Overworking
Practical Manifesting: Turning Dreams into Reality in 2025
Jurassic Pharaohs: Unlocking the Magick of Ancient Egypt and Dino Wicca
The Happiness Equation: Small Changes for Big Joy
The Confidence Compass: Finding Your Inner Strength
Whispers in the Hollow: Tales of the Forgotten Beasts
Echoes from the Hollow: The Return of Forgotten Beasts
The Hollow Ascendant: The Rise of the Forgotten Beasts
The Relationship Reset: Building Better Connections
Mastering the Morning: How to Win the Day Before 8 AM
The Shadow's Dance: Groundhog Day Symbolism
Cupid's Kitchen: Quick Valentine's Day Recipes
Valentine's Day on a Budget: Love Without Breaking the Bank
Astrocraft: Aligning the Stars in the World of Minecraft
Forecasting Life: Groundhog Day Reflections

Bleeding Hearts: Twisted Tales of Valentine's Terror

Herbal Smoke Revolution: The Ultimate Guide to Nature's Cigarette Alternative

Winter's Wrath: The Complete Survival Blueprint for Extreme Freezes.

The Groundhog's Shadow: A Tale of Seasons
Burrowed Insights: Wisdom from the Groundhog

Sensual Strings: The Art of Erotic Bondage
Whispered Flames: Unlocking the Power of Fire Play
Forgotten Shadows: A Guide to Cryptids Lost to Time
Six Weeks of Secrets: Groundhog Day's Hidden Messages
Shadows and Cycles: Groundhog Day Reflections
The Art of Love Letters: Crafting the Perfect Message
Romantic Getaways at Home: Turning Your Space into Paradise
Purrfect Brews: A Cat Lover's Guide to Coffee and Companionship
The Groundhog's Wisdom: Timeless Lessons for Modern Life
The Shadow Oracle: Groundhog Day as a Predictor
Emerging from the Burrow: A Journey of Renewal
The Language of Love: Learning Your Partner's Love Style
Authorpreneur: The Ultimate Blueprint for Writing, Publishing, and Thriving as an Author
Weathering the Seasons: Groundhog Day Perspectives
Valentine's Day Magic: A Guide to Romantic Rituals
The Shadow Chronicles: Stories of Groundhog Day
Love and Laughter: Fun Games for Valentine's Day
AstroRealty: Unlocking the Stars for Property Success
The Groundhog's Path: A Guide to Seasonal Balance
Groundhog Day Diaries: Reflections in the Shadow
The Groundhog's Light: Illuminating the Path Ahead
Valentine's Traditions from Around the World
AI Wealth Revolution: Unlocking the Trillionaire Mindset
Love Rekindled: Reigniting Passion in Relationships
Single and Thriving: Self-Love on Valentine's Day
Emerald Legends: Mystical Tales of Ireland
Green Alchemy: Harnessing Nature's Magic
The Hearts of Horror: A Valentine's Day Nightmare
The Leprechaun's Guide to Wealth and Wisdom
Dancing with the Sidhe: Celebrating the Otherworld

Shamrocks and Shadows: Mysteries of the Green Isle

Emerald Energy: Harnessing Luck and Growth

The Gingerbread Golem's Valentine: A Sweetheart's Guide to Love and Enchantment

The Celtic Knot: Weaving Life and Destiny

Green Fire: Elemental Magic for St. Patrick's Day

Clover Chronicles: Finding Your Inner Luck

Ireland's Mystical Creatures: A Field Guide

Gingerbread Golem's Love Almanac

Prowl and Thrive: The Lion's Guide to Success

Love Alchemy: Transforming Your Life Through Heart Energy

WORLD DOMINATION: Woman's Rule 3:The New Life

The Midnight Rose: A Guide to Lunar Love Spells

The Forbidden Letters: Writing Your Own Love Prophecy

Luck and Lore: St. Patrick's Day for Modern Mystics

The Green Path: A Pagan Celebration of Renewal

The Dark Architect's Guide to Reprogramming Reality

Prankster's Paradise: A Guide to Harmless Hijinks

Manifest Your Reality: The Law of Attraction Simplified

The TARDIS Owner's Manual: Understanding the Doctor's Ship: *A complete guide to the TARDIS, its technology, secrets, and mysteries*

Starlit Romance: Astrology Secrets for Finding True Love

The Time Lord's Atlas: A Complete Guide to the Whoniverse: ***A breakdown of the locations, planets, and dimensions explored in Doctor Who***

Sweetheart Shadows: The Dark Side of Love and Attraction

February Fire: Reigniting Passion in Every Area of Life

The Self-Love Toolkit: 5 Ways to Embrace Who You Are

February Sparks: Ignite Your Dreams in 28 Days

March to Success: A 31-Day Action Blueprint

Ancient Paths: The 13 Sacred Principles of Dino Wicca

Echoes of Tomorrow: Navigating the AI Revolution
The Wellness Blueprint: Balancing Mind, Body, and Soul
Green Horizons: Sustainable Living for a Better Tomorrow
The AI Wealth Code: How to Make Millions with Automation
AI-Powered Creativity: Writing, Art, and Music for Profit
Extinction Rites: Rebirthing Your Soul Through Prehistoric Magick
Sacred Serpents tarot
Celestial Enchantment blank journal
Star Strains
Culinary Journeys: Exploring Global Flavors at Home
The Hollowvale Curse
The Hollowvale Harvest
The Egg of Transformation: Awakening Your Inner Power
Blooming Into Power: A Wiccan Guide to Spring Awakening
The Nightmare Nexus: The Third Doctor's Perilous Haunting
Digital Detox: Reclaiming Your Life in a Connected World
Ostara's Path: Walking the Spiral of Renewal
The Sacred Hare
Financial Freedom: Building Wealth in the Modern Age
Spring's Cauldron: Stirring the Waters of Change
The Hollowvale Pact
Quantum Consciousness: The Science of Reality Shifting
The Hollowvale Hunger
The Sacred Waters Within: A Witch's Guide to Hydrocephalus Magick
The Raven's Nest: Building a Life of Unshakable Stability
AI and the Human Mind: The Future of Intelligence
The Hollowvale Reckoning
Timeless Love: Building and Maintaining Lasting Relationships
The Raven's Roar: Unlocking Unstoppable Confidence
Raven Sight: Awakening Intuition and Inner Wisdom

The Butterfly Effect: Small Changes, Big Transformations

Taming the Boogeyman: How to Conquer Your Inner Fears

The Magick of Green: Awakening Earth's Energy in You

The Entrepreneurial Mindset: Secrets to Business Success

The Hollowvale End

The Shadow Luck Ritual: Reclaiming Power from Your Dark Side

Spring Magick for Beginners: A Simple Guide to Seasonal Energy Work

Doctor Who: The Hollowvale Conundrum

The March of Miracles: Unlocking Synchronicities in Spring

Unveiling the Cosmos: A Guide to Stargazing and Space Exploration

The Ultimate Guide to Surviving an Economic Collapse

The AI Gold Rush: How to Profit from the AI Revolution

Bastet's Shadow: The Hidden Power of Feline Magick

The Bastet Codex: Unlocking the Goddess's Magickal Secrets

Purring Spells: Harnessing Bastet's Healing Frequencies

Bastet's Nine Lives: Rebirth, Transformation, and Immortality Spells

Primal Currents: Hydrocephalus Magick in the Path of Dino Wicca

The Digital Gold Rush: Mastering E-Commerce and Online Sales

Future Shock: Adapting to the Next Decade of Change

The Quantum Mindset: Think Like a Billionaire

Sacred Motherhood: Awakening the Divine Feminine Within

The Mother's Spellbook: Enchantments for Love, Protection, and Prosperity

The Witch's Guide to Parenting: Raising Empowered and Intuitive Children

The Magick of Motherhood: Reclaiming Your Power Through Rituals

The Pagan Path to Self-Love: A Goddess's Guide to Worth and Confidence
Wild Woman Magick: Unleashing Your Primal Power
The Money Magnet Blueprint: Unlocking Unlimited Wealth
Biohacking 101: Unlock Your Body's Full Potential
The Wild Father: A Pagan Guide to Strength and Wisdom
The Sacred Masculine: Unlocking Your Inner Power
The Druid's Compass
The Warrior's Mindset
The Father's Fire
Odin's Path
Ancestral Bonds
The House That Whispers
The Magician's Code
The Wild Hunt
The Green Man's Path
The Altar of Success
The Shadow and the Sword
The High Priestess's Guide to Energy Healing
The Lunar Mother
The Sacred Self-Care Grimoire
The Womb Wisdom Codex
The Wheel of the Mother
The Witch's Guide to Manifestation
The Q2 Reset
The Ultimate Guide to AI-Powered Passive Income
Escape the 9-5
AI Feline Fortunes
The Tear-Stained Grimoire
Razorblade Runes
Cemetery Sirens
The Midnight Wristwatch
The Town That Forgets

AI Horror & Creepypasta
The Hollow Frequency
The Breach Echo
The Quiet Between Worlds
The Sigil of Tharan-Khul
Summon the Vault of Y'ha'ten
The Becoming Codex
The Profit of Az'ra-nar
The Drowned Logos
Echoes of the Eldritch Will
The Deep Ledger
Necronomicon of Networth
Covenant of the Wealthwyrm
The Whisperer's Manifesto
The Rites of Azh-K'luth
The Ark of the Crawling Coin
The Tithe of Shadows
Inkheart Abyss
The Timewinds of Y'ha-nthlei
The Spiral Labyrinth of Azag-Nirrh
The Gallifreyan Heresy of the Black Pharaoh
The Psalms of Nyog-Sotha
Black Rain Alchemy
The Infinite Maw
The Entropic Blueprint
The Oracle of Sh'guul
The Book of Breach
The Drowned Saint's Testament
Dreamcraft of the Sleeper God
The Silence Market
Cthonomics: The Dark Wealth Algorithm
Invocation of the Ten-Eyed King
Wealthbound to the Wyrm Below

Become the Unnameable
Codex of the Sovereign Flame
Rituals of Relentless Becoming
The Shadow Ascends
The Eyes Beneath You
The Will That Wakes Worlds
Silence Is a Weapon
The Mirror That Screams
The Whisper Between Moments
The Mind That Devours Fear
The Myth of the Finished Self
The Architect of Your Madness
The Voice You've Buried
The Discipline of Madness
Stormborn: Awakening Your Inner Tempest
The Mind That Ate Time
Unbind Your Becoming
The Pact You Owe Yourself
The Devourer's Diet
The Acid That Carves the Path
The Tower You Must Burn
The Breath Between Worlds
Speak Like the Deep
The Labyrinth Within
The Spine of the Sea God
Rejection Is a Portal
The Crown You Refused
The Scar Is the Spell
The Lightless Flame
The Habit of Becoming Horrific
ChickenJockey Chaos
The Gatekeeper Within
You Are Not Your Name

The Compass of the Mad
The Archive of Unsent Letters
What the Mirror Can't Show You
The Knife You Needed
Worship Nothing, Become Everything
The Other Voice
The Body the World Forgot
The Vein of the Void
The Black Bone Codex
The Puzzle of the Hidden Self (Millennium Puzzle)
The Eye That Sees the Lie *(Millennium Eye)*
The Ring of Return (Millennium Ring)
The Rod of Relentless Will ***(Millennium Rod)***
The Tally of the Soul (Millennium Tauk/Necklace)
The Key to the Locked Timeline (Millennium Key)
The Scale of Sacred Decisions (Millennium Scales)
Inferno Bites: The UnOfficial Minecraft Lava Cookbook
Rot in the Attic
Prana: The Hidden Force of Your Infinite Self
The Shadow Realm Within: Transforming Darkness Into Destiny
The Borderland Collapse
Claws of Protection: Bastet's Defensive Magick
Mr. Ring-a-Ding's Madness
Yugioh Astrology: Celestial Deckcraft and Duel Destiny (2026–2027 Edition)
The Seal You Signed: Unlocking the Power You Once Feared
The Puzzle of Infinite Minds: Unlocking the Mentalism Hidden Within
The Eye That Mirrors the All: Secrets of Inner Reflection
Doctor Who: The Toymaker's Broadcast
The Rod of Eternal Flow: Commanding the Currents of Vibration

Golden Eyes of Bastet: Enhancing Psychic Vision
The Key of Dual Forces: Balance Within the Polarity
The Scales of Living Rhythm: Timing the Dance of Life
The Necklace of Hidden Cause: Weaving the Webs of Fate
The Ring of Secret Masters: Rising Through the All Within All
Daggers of the Dying Deep
Bastet's Wealth and Fortune Magick: Prosperity Rituals of the Goddess
The Tide that Speaks
The Scrolls of Petosiris: 13 Rituals from the Feathered Eye
Petosiris and the Living Plague of Osirion
Feline Fire: Bastet's Passion and Love Magick
The Star Altar of Petosiris
Bastet's Whiskers: Supernatural Sensory Magick
The Bastet Grimoire
Feeding the Shadows
The Mouthless Prayer
The Spiral Wound
Becoming the Ibis: Lessons from Petosiris's Mind
The Crimson Coven: Cola Magick for Sweet Dominion
Sacred Cat's Paw
The Soda Zodiac: A Flavor for Every Sign
Covenant of the Crawling Flame
The Ink of Ish'Zur
Frothroot: The Thirst That Ate the World
The Golden Glyphs of Prosperity
The Etherbind Codex
Echoes of the Resistance: Reclaiming the You That Survived
Harnessed Minds: Breaking Free from Mental Control
The Eyes in the Smoke
Rootwake: The Carbon Covenant
Skitter Logic: Unlearning the Fear That Built You

Doctor Who: The World That Froths
Rootwake: The Fizz That Rewrites Flesh
Rootwake: Frothfather of the World
The Holly Pact: Blood Beneath the Mistletoe
The 2nd Mass Principle: Building Unbreakable Tribes
Web of Wits: A Survival Guide to Encounters with Anasi the Spider (Aunt Nancy)
The Hexbreaking Handbook: Effective Spells to Remove Curses
Pop Alchemy: Transform Your Life One Sip at a Time
The Mason Code: Leading in Unleadable Times
Petosiris and the Fifth Chamber of Thoth
The Ether Seed Within
The Parent of Tomorrow
Petosiris's Pyramid of Perpetual Wealth
Unlearn the World
Grimoire of the Hollow Tongue
Zodiac Weeds: Finding Your Strain Through the Stars
Aquarius Rises in the Bank
The Sugar God's Smile
The Skinclock Reversal: Biohacking the Face of Time
Debtburn: How to Obliterate What You Owe Forever
The Ice Cream Oracle: What Your Cone Says About Your Future
Silence Is Sovereignty: The Power of Being Unreadable
The Wind That Whispers Through Stone
Path of the Four Directions
Doctor Who: The Maestro's Symphony of Endings
Oxygen Grail: Breathing to Undo the Clock
Zodiacal Collapse: When Stars Devour Time
Teachings from the Red Sand Silence
Doctor Who: Omega – The Broken Equation
Memory Wipe Your Past: Start Over Like a MiB

Mitochondria Prime: Ignite the Core of Youth
A Nest of Roaches
Grub from the Galaxy: MiB Recipes You'll Never Forget
Whiskers of Power: Bastet's Guide to Inner Sovereignty
The Gift Must Cost Them: Negotiation Through Unequal Exchange
The Worm Guys' Wealth Code: Hustle Like an Alien
Bug Out: The Edgar Method for Ruthless Goal Setting
Weaving Life with Spiderwoman's Pattern
Doctor Who: The Rani's Renaissance
How to Get a Job (If You're a Puppygirl)
Speak Through Others: The Art of Proxy Power
T-Rex Your Trauma: Reclaim the Power of Your Primal Self
The Black Briefcase: How MiB Stay Wealthy in Silence
The Thirst Beyond Reason: Understanding Diabetes Insipidus From the Inside Out
Backwoods Witchcraft for Billionaires: The Pagan Path from Dirt Roads to Gold Roads
The Moonshine Grimoire: Fermented Spells for Abundance
The Nameless Geometry
The Wraith's Mixtape: Spellcasting with Songs of Sorrow
The Gallifreyan Gentleman: Silent Wealth, Sonic Confidence, and the Doctor's Code of Living
Sugar Water Confidence
Dino Totems: Spirit Guides from Earth's First Gods
Pumpkin Sigils & Ritual Smoke
The Hózhó Compass
The Distortus Discipline – Order from Inner Mutation
Witchcraft for the Cold-Blooded Soul
Moonlight Over the Blessingway
Water, Interrupted: When the Body Forgets How to Hold On
Deformed but Divine: Embracing Your Asymmetry
Hexes in the Henhouse: The Farm Witch's Guide to Power

The Reversed Flame: A Grimoire of Inverted Power

Salt, Cells, and Sanity: Reclaiming Balance with Diabetes Insipidus

King of the Broken: Crowning the Flawed Self

Moonlight Scars: Emo Moon Magick and the Art of Lunar Sorrow

Noose Spells: Magick of the Hanging Rope

The Goth Cathedral: Rituals of the Broken and Beautiful

The Cretaceous Codex: Dino Spirits and Fossil Magick

The Turkey Bones Ritual

Nine Lives of Manifestation: Unlocking Bastet's Reality Codes

Chaos Muscles: Building Strength from Twisted Pain

Emo Blood Magick: The Veins of Power

The 3AM Flood: Nighttime Urination, Sleep Loss, and the DI Spiral

The Silence Between the Stars

The Lemon Method: Sour Your Way to Success

Starlit Sovereign

The Rite of Twelve Gates: Walking the Gates of the Duat.

Cornbread and Conjure: Recipes for Riches and Rootwork

The Black Rose Rituals: Emo Love Spells and Obsession Magick

The Eternal Goodbye: Death Magick and Rebirth Rituals

Sinkrot: The Drain That Remembers

The Hybrid Mindset: Thinking Beyond Evolution

Bone Dry: Navigating Dehydration Before It Breaks You

Wreathcraft: Winter Sigils and Yuletide Spells

The Rite of Twelve Mouths

S'mores of the Damned: Haunted Recipes for Halloween Night

Rethink the Drink: A Beverage Survival Guide for DI Warriors

The Shadow Chord: Guitar Magick and Sonic

Malformed Yet Majestic: Leading When You Feel Wrong Inside
The Cursed Diary: Ink-Stained Spells of the Emo Soul
Anxiety Off Switch: Emergency Reset for a Fried Nervous System
The Energy Heist: How to Take Back Your Life from Drainers
Beyond the Bathroom: Rebuilding Your Social Life With DI
Coyote's Gift for Decision Makers
Ghoul-Goo: Spooky S'mores You'll Die For
Echoes in the Mirror: Scrying and Self-Destruction Magick
Thread and Thorn: Stitching Spells from Rural Cloth
The Mogwai Mind: Building Untouchable Wealth from Small Ideas
Be Your Own Guide: Trust Your Inner Compass
Hormones in Chaos: The Endocrine Puzzle of Diabetes Insipidus
ChronoCleanse: Detox Your Biological Timeline
The Limb You Hide Is the One That Saves You
Leaves, Bones, and Whisper Spells
The Dinosaur Mindset: Prehistoric Tactics for Modern Wealth
Clawing Back Control: A Bastet Method for Boundaries and Empowerment
Samhain Codes of the Forgotten
Orange Alchemy: The Autumnal Spellbook
Monster Within, Master Without
The Sigil That Sleeps
Hearthcraft: Yule Hearth Sigils and Winter Warmth Spells
Temple of the Purring Moon: Rituals from Bastet's Lineage
When the Earth Remembers Your Footsteps
Food for Mood: Eat to Heal Depression, Not Just Survive It
Witch of the Kudzu Vine: Southern Pagan Wealth Secrets
The Invisible Diagnosis: Advocating for Yourself With DI

The Coffin's Lullaby: Sleep Magick and Nightmares as Portals
Ashes of the Will: Rituals for Erasing the Self
The Fracture Rite: Shattering the Magickal Core
Funeral Candles: The Art of Emo Flame Magick
The Black Grimoire: A Blank Ritual for Writing in Absence
Phantom Thirst: A Halloween Survival Guide for Diabetes Insipidus
The Hollow Crown: Emo Royalty and Magick of the Outcast King
Sandpainting for the Soul
Falling Into Balance: Using the Extra Hour to Recalibrate Life
100 Southern Superstitions That Still Work
The DI Child: A Parent's Guide to Raising Hydrated, Happy Kids
The Jungle of Shame: Escaping the Hidden Lab of Doubt
The Witch's Toast: S'mores Spells and Creepy Confections
The Hoodoo Pantry: Spells from the Mason Jar
The Immortal Fortune: Secret Wealth Lessons from Captain Jack Harkness
The Specter's Embrace: Magick for Channeling Ghostly Lovers
Grateful Waters: A Thanksgiving Survival Guide for Diabetes Insipidus
The Seizure Gospel
Harvestbind: Autumn Sigils and Samhain Spells
Doctor Who: The Algorithmic Awakening
Silent Nights, Steady Waters: A Christmas Survival Guide for Diabetes Insipidus
The Extra Hour Effect: How One Hour Can Transform Everything
Blade Between the Breaths
Running with the Mountain Shadows
Echoes of the Failed Experiment – Becoming a Living Legacy

Swamp Witches & River Ghosts: Real Southern Hauntings

Cornbread Prophecies: Magical Recipes from a Southern Table

Doctor Who: The Signal in the Star

Bloomcraft: Spring Sigils and Equinox Enchantments

Vanisher: How to Disappear from the Internet Without Losing Your Life

The Ultimate Christmas Cookie Cookbook

The Unbreakable Parent: How to Mentally Survive Raising Kids in a Broken World

Time Debt: How to Reclaim the Hours You Didn't Know You Lost

One Month, One Million: Unconventional Cash Creation Tactics

Doctor Who: The Cyber Conversion Protocol

Black Friday Frenzy: The Art of Finding Hidden Online Deals

The Grimoire Buried Under the Apple Tree

Digital Couponing Masterclass: Your Step-by-Step Guide to Black Friday Savings

The Fire Inside the Flint

Shadows on the Ceiling: The Emo Guide to Astral Magick

The Bone-Eaters Beneath Us

Black Friday Bundle Blueprint: Creating Irresistible Product Packages for Maximum Sales

Thirteen Nights of Unbinding

Doctor Who: Engines of Influence

Pumpkin Spice Alchemy: Recipes of Fire and Frost

When Raptor Met Rexy: Prehistoric Lessons in Wild Romance

Oblivion's Candle: Burn the Path Behind You

Campfire Curses and Chocolate: A Halloween S'mores Grimoire

The Wallet That Wasn't Mine: Breaking Free from Inherited Scarcity
The Cola Zodiac: What Your Fizz Says About Your Fate
Frostfire Fortune: Unlocking Winter's Hidden Prosperity
Signal Jamming: Detox Your Brain from Info Overload
The Dust of the Forgotten Rite
The Golden Cat Sigils: Drawing Power in Bastet's Name
Mud Magick: The Prosperity of Getting Dirty
Savory Spicefall: Beyond the Pumpkin Pie
Pumpkin Spice Apothecary Kitchen
The Pumpkin Spice Economy: Turning Trends into Billions
The Ember Veil: 13 Nights of Fire Magick
Financial Freeze: When Earning Triggers Panic
The Gingerbread Alchemist: Sweet Recipes with a Twist
Biosynth Power: Programming Yourself from Scratch
Echoes from the Talking Circle
Truffle Alchemy: Fungus of Fortune
Spores of Power: The Truffle Witch's Handbook
Doctor Who: The Tower That Speaks
The Mycelium Veil: Truffle Magick Unbound
Broke But Ashamed: Healing the Shame Wound of Debt
The Evergreen Mind: Growth Through Winter Stillness
The Black Veil Truffle Rite
The Voice Beneath Symbols
Witchlight on the Bayou: Swamp Spells for Sovereignty
I Grew Up Poor and Now I Sabotage My Success
The Lantern of Hollow Souls
Shutdown Survival: A Citizen's Guide to Thriving When Government Stops
When Abundance Feels Like a Threat: Healing the Hidden Fears of Enough
The Scarecrow Grimoire
Owls of the October Veil

Candlewax and Curses: A Halloween Spellbook

Excavating the Inner Fossil – Transforming Fossilized Thoughtforms into Tools of Power

The Yule Witch's Spellbook: Magick for the Holiday Season

Haunted Christmas: Ghost Stories for Winter Nights

The Christmas Survival Guide: Thriving Through the Chaos

The Bone Orchard Rites

Haunted Commerce: The Ghost in the Marketplace

When Money Triggers the Inner Child

Silent Night with the Silence: A Christmas Thriller

The Lightning Crown: Living and Leading Through Seizures

TARDIS Tidings: Festive Stories from the Whoniverse

Autumn Reset: Slowing Down Without Falling Behind

The Trillion Dollar Soul: Rewriting the Currency of Reality

Truffle Eclipse Magick

Micro-Manifestations: Quick Magick That Works

5-Minute Rituals for Busy Witches

The Marshmallow Massacre: Halloween Treats with a Sinister Twist

Blood and Blackberry Thorns

Magickal Mornings: Rituals for a Blessed Christmas Day

Embers of the All-Hallows Fire

The Pumpkin Market Collapse

The Hour You Gained: Transforming Time Into Power

The Chamber Must Be Sealed: Mastering the Power of Controlled Access

The Cursed Manuscript of Petosiris

The Festive Hearth: Creating Holiday Traditions

Darkness Rising: Thriving as Nights Grow Longer

Harvesting Time: Turning the Year's End Into Your New Beginning

Petosiris and the 13th Zodiac Key

Wagewound: When Paychecks Become Identity Prisons

Walls That Watch

The Silent Feast: Rituals of Power in the Longest Night

The Distortus Legacy : Becoming a Deformed King in a Perfect World

The Hollow Masks

The Gratitude Furnace: Forging Gold from Thanks

Feast of Inner Gold: Eating for Energy and Enlightenment

Haunted Commerce: The Season of Spending Spirits

Fear Bonds: How Panic Creates Profit

Black Friday E-Commerce Playbook: Sales Tactics to Skyrocket Your Holiday Revenue

Budgeting for Black Friday: A Holiday Savings Planner

Haunting the Harvest Moon

The Warrior's Water: Emergency Preparedness for People With DI

The First Sip of the Year: A New Year's Survival Guide for Diabetes Insipidus

Doctor Who: The Thirteenth Node

The Unseen Struggle: Mental Health, Anxiety, and Chronic Thirst

The Hearth's Hidden Ledger: Counting Energies as Currency

The Gift Alchemist: Turning Any Offering Into Gold

The Papyrus of the Bound Spirit

The Magick of Leftovers: Transmutation in the Fridge

Frost and Fortune: Christmas Wealthcraft for the Modern Magus

Last-Minute Gifts: Creative Ideas on a Budget

10 Secrets to Surviving Holiday Crowds

The Witch's Dow Jones

The Witches' Graveyard Shift

Pumpkin Sigils: Carving Rites for Midnight Power

The Secret Shopper's Black Friday Guide: How to Get Early Access and VIP Deals

Fever in the Foundation
The Neuralyzer Reset: Reprogram Your Morning Routine
Lightning Lessons of the White Painted Woman
The Enchanted Snowflake
The Magic Sip: Surviving Disney Parks with Diabetes Insipidus
The One Who Draws Through You
Santa's Secrets: A Magical Holiday Planner
Silent Bells, Loud Miracles: Self-Help for the Season of Stillness
The Sugar Spell Codex: Confectionary Magick of Christmas
Autumn Hexcraft: Fallen Leaves, Fallen Barriers
Sleep Like a Fortress: Build a Life Where Insomnia Can't Survive
Nowhere Was Ever Home
Christmas Under the Stars: A Celestial Holiday Guide
Rentproof: How to Never Be Evicted Again
Workless: Escape the 9-5 Without Being Broke
The Gilded Gift: A Wealth Altar for Christmas Morning
The Black Friday Grimoire
The Hollowing: Ceremonies of Spiritual Collapse
Doctor Who: The Nameless Signal
Where the Eagle Hides His Courage
The Dwarf Tyrant's Ascent: Claiming Power in a World of Giants

Get Some Tarot cards: https://www.makeplayingcards.com/sell/apophis-occult-shop

Get some shirts: https://www.bonfire.com/store/apophis-shirt-emporium/

Instagrams:
@apophis_enterprises,
@apophisbookemporium,
@apophisscardshop
Twitter: @apophisenterpr1
Tiktok:@apophisenterprise
Youtube: @sg1fan23477
Hive: @sg1fan23477
CheeLee: @SG1fan23477

Podcast: Apophis Chat Zone: https://open.spotify.com/show/5zXbrCLEV2xzCp8ybrfHsk?si=fb4d4fdbdce44dec

Newsletter: https://apophiss-newsletter-27c897.beehiiv.com/

If you want to support me or see posts of other projects that I have come over to: **buymeacoffee.com/mpetchinskg**

I post there daily several times a day

Get your Dinowicca or Christmas themed digital products, especially Santa Raptor songs and other musics. Here: **https://sg1fan23477.gumroad.com**

Apophis Yuletide Digital has not only digital Christmas items, but it will have all things with Dinowicca as well as other Digital products.

www.ingramcontent.com/pod-product-compliance
Lightning Source LLC
LaVergne TN
LVHW020235210926
848481LV00016B/2335